SBN 361 02854 7
Copyright © 1974 Purnell & Sons Limited
Published by Purnell Books, Berkshire House,
Queen Street, Maidenhead
Made and printed in Great Britain by
Purnell & Sons Limited, Paulton (Somerset) and
London

# Pony
# Magazine Annual 1975

### Edited by Michael Williams

**PURNELL**

# Contents

# Foreword

**G**lancing back through some of the earlier annuals it seems that every year has brought some change from the last; and this, I suspect, reflects the growing demands of our young, and not-so-young, readers. The 1975 annual is no exception; the most notable change for some being the omission of that famous pair, Pat and Pickles, who, after spending no fewer than 23 years escapading through the pages of PONY, have gracefully retired. However, we are now including some 'seasonal' cartoons by Janet Slade, which I know you will enjoy, and a new "Did You Know?" section, revealing some amazing facts and figures about horses.

More often than not, it seems, the letters from readers that arrive in our office contain a plea for more of the "Enquiry Bureau" and "Vet to the Rescue" columns of the magazine, telling us how useful they have been. So this year we asked our veterinary correspondent if he would like to contribute to the annual and he has produced a good, factual article on caring for a pony living out. To keep the balance, and for those of you who keep or look after stabled ponies, Veronica Riches runs through the daily routine that should be followed. In addition, to help you with your riding, Jane Strachan explains why early riding lessons do not always go as smoothly as they might.

And, of course, we have lots of intriguing and sometimes hilarious stories by your favourite authors—including Caroline Akrill and Josephine Pullein-Thompson, plus many photographs and the usual round of puzzles, quizzes and competitions.

We do hope that you will enjoy this 1975 edition of PONY's own annual and here's wishing you all a lovely Christmas and a lucky new year.

# What Was A Horse?

by **Sally Dudley**

illustrated by **Nicola Palin**

Andrek came into the sitting-room, thought himself up a chair from the city memory bank and sat down.

"Father?"

"Yes, Andrek."

"What was a horse?"

"A horse?" He looked puzzled.

"Yes."

"I've never heard of one. Was it some kind of fruit?"

"It may have been, I don't really know."

"Why don't you go down to central computer, son? It should know. Where did you hear of . . . a horse?"

"The history computer used the word," Andrek explained.

"Oh. Well, off you go."

Andrek stood up. The chair disappeared and he thought a door. He stepped through it and it disappeared too. Andrek stepped onto the path outside and was whisked away.

A few minutes later he stepped off into a large circular building which was topped by a domed roof. Andrek walked to one out of many seats, each in front of a screen, sat down and put on a helmet.

It was a simple system. You simply thought the question, and the answer appeared on the screen. Words and diagrams would appear, together with a list of cassettes dealing with the subject.

"What was a horse?" Andrek thought.

The computer hesitated fractionally, then a series of pictures appeared on the screen, with the word 'Animal' beside them. It had four long, thin legs topped by a cylindrical body. One end tapered and a head was on top. The upper part of this 'neck', as Andrek saw it, was covered with long hair. There was a lump or bundle of longer hair at the other end, and the whole creature was covered with short hairs. Andrek studied it in amazement.

"Are you sure that is a horse?"

"Yes," answered the computer.

"What was it used for?"

"Pleasure. People used to place a special seat on its back . . ."

A picture of a saddle appeared, and the computer said: ". . . and it was controlled by a collection of straps on its head." An image of a bridle came up on the screen.

"People sat on the saddle, as the seat was called, with a leg down each side, the foot resting on the platform, as you can see . . ."

A picture then appeared of someone mounted.

"They steered and stopped by the two longest straps, which they held in their hands."

"Did they eat it?" questioned Andrek.

"Only very rarely. Most people loved them too much. But despite this, horses are now extinct."

There was a slight pause. Then, "That's all the information I have."

Andrek removed the helmet and went home.

"Well, son?"

"It's an animal with four legs. People used to sit on them like scooters and steer them using straps. But now they're extinct."

*"Are you sure that is a horse?"*

9

# The Right Of The Line

*by Norman Dodd*

**The King's Troop Royal Horse Artillery in action.**

Thousands of spectators at the Royal Tournament and at many shows throughout Britain are thrilled every year by the spectacular Musical Drive performed by the King's Troop of the Royal Horse Artillery. But few know much about the history and background of this famous Troop or of the amount of hard work which goes on behind the scenes in the training of the horses and in keeping them 'galloping fit' at all times.

I was fortunate enough to spend a day at their stables and barracks in St. John's Wood, London, and to be shown round by the Adjutant, Captain G. T. C. Musgrave RHA, who answered my many questions.

The Troop, he told me, has 185 officers, NCOs and Gunners, six guns and 111 horses. Although everyone is a trained soldier, the duties of the Troop are mainly ceremonial. They are responsible for firing salutes on the Royal Birthdays, for visiting Heads of State and on other special occasions. One of the gun teams draws the gun limber which carries the coffin at State funerals; a sombre task which requires considerable steadiness in the horses as they move through the London crowds. It is, however, for their displays that they are best known by the public and it is for these that the training, both for the horses and men, is the hardest. It takes fit and courageous men and horses to carry out the intricate figures of eight at the full gallop in an enclosed arena; there is no room for mistakes.

The soldiers mostly enlist from the 'riding fraternity'. Prospective recruits are invited to spend a few days with the Troop; if they are considered suitable and still wish to join, they are enlisted and carry out normal recruit training as members of the Royal Artillery. After this they go to the Troop and are given intensive riding training in the military style. This entails learning to ride with much longer leathers than are normally used by stable lads and even by the show jumpers. As bucket-type cavalry saddles are used, the seat must be well with the horse at all paces.

Drivers must learn to handle their own horses using one hand for the reins while steadying the second paired horse and keeping it up to its traces. This is not so easy for the wheel driver, who has his off-side leg in a re-inforced 'boot' to protect it from the pressure of the pole of the limber. Every soldier must learn all about stable management, the proper care of their tack, balanced feeding, grooming to fit the horses for the Queen herself, and the simple ailments of horses.

Captain Musgrave said that many recruits had first to unlearn what they thought they knew about riding and horses, though some experience in the handling of animals could be useful. The length of the riding course depends upon previous experience but it is usually two to four years before pupils qualify for the élite position of driver in one of the teams.

Many men stay a long time with the Troop, enjoying the riding and the hard life of an élite soldier. Master Saddler S/Sgt. Richard King has been with the Troop for 19 years. BSM Eric Witts, the senior riding instructor, has 18 years service with the Troop behind him, and has represented the unit in many jumping competitions. S/Sgt. Ben Jones was in the British Olympic team and won a gold medal. Colonel Frank Weldon, one of Britain's greatest horsemen, was once the Commanding Officer and to-day trains the British team. He uses the Troop's saddler to check all the Olympic equipment before and during the competitions. The tack of the Troop itself is a joy to behold! It has to be perfect, for men's lives depend upon it; there is a nice tradition in the saddle room: each set of

**The March Past.**

equipment hangs under the name of the driver in that position in E Battery RHA at the Battle of Waterloo in 1815.

The Troop is also self-contained for all farrier's work. There are five farriers in the unit who work under the control of Master Farrier Sgt. Cyril Morgan, who accompanied the British Three-Day Event team to the Olympic Games in Mexico and Munich and the 1973 European Championships at Kiev.

Virtually all the horses are purchased in Ireland by the Royal Army Veterinary Corps Purchasing Commission. The Troop produces an annual 'shopping list' by sizes and colours required. There are six sub-sections, each of six horses; one is light bay, two bay, two brown and one black; and, of course, they must all match. These horses are all termed 'ride and drive' and have no special pedigrees. The chargers used by the officers and senior NCOs are better-class and average 17 hands, the gun team horses being only 15.2. The latter must be tough; the lead horses are the strongest because they do proportionately more of the pulling, while the wheelers, who are the brakes, have to be smaller with rounded rumps to do the breeching to stop the 1½ tons of guns and limber behind them.

The chargers, which cost about £375, and the team horses, which cost about £300, are bought as five-year-olds and normally are not 'backed'; this is done at the Troop. On arrival the horses are trained up to the standard that they can be ridden on parade the following year, but they are not usually included in a gun team until the year after. All horses have to be thoroughly fit and there are well-appointed sick lines for any who have temporary illnesses. However, most of them keep in excellent condition, partly owing to the care lavished on them by their riders and handlers. Many of these men get very fond of their mounts and some find the money to buy them when they are cast. From 15 years onwards each horse is carefully examined annually, and if no longer up to the gruelling work of the Troop it is suitably disposed of, sometimes to other Cavalry regiments which do not have to tow guns, sometimes to the RAVC Depot for use in riding instruction. A few go to recognised Army Saddle Clubs, some have to be destroyed painlessly; and sometimes permission is given for them to be bought out.

The Troop is fortunate in having one of the largest enclosed riding schools in London. Built in 1824, it is still going strong. If you are around St. John's Wood early in the morning you will often see the horses in the streets, with a soldier riding one of them and leading two others. The soldiers are encouraged to ride their horses in shows, to follow drag hounds, and to take part in all types of equestrian sports. It may sound a wonderful life to be paid to ride horses, but it is also hard work to keep 'on top' for every day of the year, rain or shine.

Why 'The King's Troop' and 'Right of the Line'? As far back as 1756, King George III officially confirmed the long-standing tradition that the Artillery, when on parade with its guns (which are the Colours of the Regiment), should parade at the Right of the Line of troops on official occasions; and so it has remained to this day even when the Guards are on parade. The Royal Horse Artillery are 'the Guards of the Gunners' and the officers and men of the King's Troop in their colourful blue and red uniforms and tall plumed busbys, which have remained unchanged since 1793, are the show-piece of the Royal Regiment.

Although there has been a battery in London since 1804, it was not until October 1947 that it gained its present title. On the first of that month, King George VI paid a visit to the Troop, which was then known as 'The Riding Troop RHA', and on signing the visitors' book after his inspection he boldly struck the word 'Riding' out of the title and wrote 'King's' in its place. From that moment on it became 'The King's Troop RHA' and at the express wish of Her Majesty The Queen it has remained so to this day.

Next time you see the Troop at a show, why not go round and visit the horses afterwards? The Gunners are always delighted to show you their charges and tell you a little about them. I was told that 13-year-old Hancock, the leader of

'F', the black sub-section, had bitten 95% of the Troop; and that Royalty, an eight-year-old mare, was the best leader in the unit — his Sub Section No 1, Sgt. Clarke, who has been with the Troop for nine years, said so, so it must be true! And also when you see them on parade, or watch their display, think of the work which goes on behind the scenes to produce the immaculate turn-out and brilliant driving which is always expected from the Troop, a King's Troop. The Right of the Line.

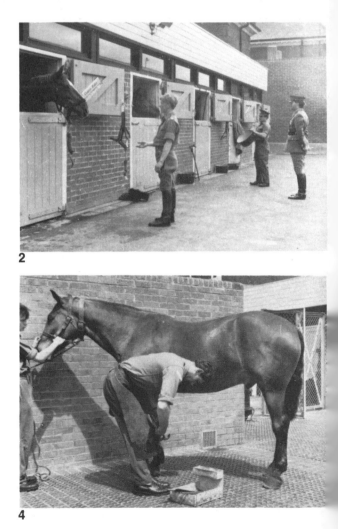

2

4

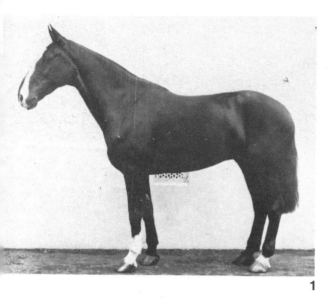

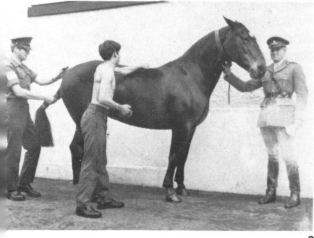

1

1. 13-year-old Hancock is the leader of 'F' Sub Section which is made up of only black horses. Horses from this section are used on State funerals.
2. The Troop's well-equipped sick lines are inspected by Captain Musgrave.
3. Lt. Jeremy Glover R.H.A., Sgt. Clarke and Gnr. Fulton, with Royalty, an 8-year-old mare who is the lead horse in 'D' Sub Section. 4. Farrier L/Bdr. Moxon shoeing Revenge, a wheeler of 'C' Sub Section. 5. The tack room: each set of equipment hangs under the name of the driver who rode the horse in that particular position at the Battle of Waterloo in 1815. 6. A typical military saddle in the saddle room. All the equipment must be kept in first-class order as men's lives may depend upon it.

3

5

6

# The Lamentable Leading Rein

*by Caroline Akrill*

**Illustrated by Elaine Roberts**

*It was a tiny grey pony with huge dark eyes. . . .*

Aunt Sybil had bought a new brood mare. We watched it unloaded. It was a tiny grey pony with huge dark eyes, a flowing mane, and a tail that almost swept the floor.

"That would make a show pony," Sarah said. "It has everything. Quality. Bone. A lovely long front. Clean limbs. And the prettiest little head I have ever seen."

"Does it move?" Simon asked.

"Let's see," Aunt Sybil said. She led the pony down the yard and trotted it back past us. We agreed that it certainly moved. It really got its hocks underneath it and threw out its toes.

"But it's too small," Becky said. "If I rode it, my feet would touch the floor."

"You couldn't show it, you idiot," Simon said. "It is only about eleven hands and not at all the type of pony one could show in the 12.2."

"What could we show it in then?" Sarah wondered. "Mountain and Moorland? Welsh Section

'A'? In-hand or ridden?"

"Well, it can't be brood mare classes yet," Aunt Sybil said. "Since it hasn't been served and won't be this time. I don't want any late foals. Still, her offspring would certainly be worth more if the mare had a bit of form behind her."

We looked the pony up and down. The pretty mare looked at us with her big dark eyes. She pricked her little ears and wondered about us, whilst we scratched our heads and nibbled our nails and wondered about her.

"I know!" we all said together. "Leading Rein!"

"We haven't got a rider," Becky said.

"Michael Grey would ride her," Sarah said.

"Who is going to lead it?" Simon enquired in a voice which implied that whoever was elected, it certainly wasn't going to be him.

"You will lead it," Aunt Sybil said firmly. "Men always appear to do the job better. They look more professional. In a dark suit, with a bowler hat and a carnation, you will look very well."

Becky and I immediately collapsed with hysteria at the mere suggestion. Simon was aghast. "Never!" he said. "I should be the laughing stock of the show-ring!"

"But you already are," Sarah pointed out. "Nobody else goes about looking like you do. Nobody wears such outlandish clothes. Nobody has hair as long as yours. People already think you are peculiar. This is your big chance to prove you are really quite normal."

"What a nice old girl you turned out to be," Simon said sarcastically.

"Come along now," Aunt Sybil said briskly. "You would only need to cut a fraction off your hair. It will soon grow again."

"It would grow stronger and thicker," Sarah said. "Think of all those split ends."

"You could change immediately you came out of the ring," I added.

"Possibly no one would even know it was you at all," Becky said, "since you would probably not be recognised."

Simon gave us all a defeated look. He was outnumbered. He was beaten, and he knew it.

We entered the pony for Windsor and began to get it ready. It was rather fat, so we stabled it and just turned it out for a few hours a day on a bare paddock, kept for such a purpose. We had her teeth and feet attended to. We lunged her with side-reins and Becky schooled her gently under saddle. We got her to move freely with a rider on top and keep her head in the right place. Then we clipped a leading rein on and taught her to walk on the end of it, to stop, walk, and trot on command. We taught her to stand for long periods and not move a muscle whilst she was felt all over, banged with catalogues and festooned with rosettes. We rode and led her in company with traffic, and we mucked her out with Radio One turned on full blast.

PMA—B

*We lunged her with side-reins. . . .*

Then we bathed and strapped her, stripped off the old winter coat, pulled her mane and tail. We trimmed her heels, ears, whiskers and throat. We stood and regarded our handiwork.

"She is a credit to you," Aunt Sybil said. "No one would believe it was the same pony. She looks beautiful."

"All we have to do now," Becky said with fiendish glee, "is to deal with Simon."

We persuaded him to sit on the mounting block. Sarah got out the trimming scissors.

"Will he sit?" Becky said. "Or do we have to tie him down?"

"If you cut too much off," Simon said grimly to Sarah, "it will be the last thing you do on this earth."

"Whoops!" Sarah said, lopping off a huge chunk level with Simon's left ear. "I think I have made a mistake. Now I shall have to cut it all to match."

"Grief!" Simon yelled, staring in anguish at the five-inch hank of hair lying on the cobbles. "I am nearly bald!"

"My hand slipped," Sarah said glibly.

"It suits you shorter," I said. "It looks nice."

"Of course it does," said Aunt Sybil. "You look almost civilised."

"We never knew you had ears," Sarah said.

"Well, I don't like it," Becky said. "I don't think it suits you at all. I think you look funny with short hair."

And she was the only one who spoke the truth.

\*　　\*　　\*　　\*　　\*　　\*

The leading rein ponies are judged on Sunday, which is the last day of the Royal Windsor Horse Show. We drove over in the horse-box in plenty of time for the preliminary judging of the class which was scheduled for two o'clock. Mrs. Grey arrived just after half past one, with Michael in the car. She screamed with laughter when she saw Simon in his best dark suit, with his short hair and a red carnation in his button-hole. Simon scowled furiously and went back into the horse-box.

"Now I have upset him," Mrs. Grey said. "I shall have to go and apologise."

"I am too hot in all these clothes," Michael said. "I'm going to take them off."

"Not until after the class you won't," Sarah said firmly.

We took off the little pony's rugs. We had already bathed and strapped her before we set out, so she was spotless. Becky chalked her legs and Sarah vaselined her nose, round her eyes, her dock and her hooves. I brushed out her tail and finished off the last plaits in her mane.

Mrs. Grey came out of the horse-box. "She looks lovely," she said admiringly. "She is sure to win the class. I have never seen such a lovely pony in all my life."

"I don't like grey ponies," Michael said. "I like them piebald or palomino."

"Nobody asked your opinion," Becky said.

"That's right," Mrs. Grey said. "Keep him well under control. Sometimes he is an impossible child." She made Michael go and sit in the horse-box in case he fell over and got his white jodhpurs dirty. "I didn't want to come anyway," he said as he climbed up the steps.

"This day will end with a murder," Becky said. "I can feel it in my bones."

We went to tell Simon the mare was ready. "It is only a quarter to two," he said. "I am not going out until the very last minute. I shall be the last one to go into the ring and hope to God I shall be the first one out."

"I can't understand your attitude really," Mrs. Grey told him. "You look a proper gentleman. It's just that it takes one rather by surprise at first."

Simon produced another red carnation and put it in the buttonhole of Michael's navy showing coat. Michael immediately screwed up his nose and pulled it out.

"It smells," he said. "It's silly. I'm not going to wear it."

"Don't be silly, dear," Mrs. Grey said. She picked up the carnation and put it back on his coat. "You must wear it. It looks lovely."

Michael looked sulky and began to fiddle with the gas fire. "We had better get out of here," Simon said wearily. "Before he blows us all up."

We tacked up the mare and clipped on the leading rein. Simon lifted Michael into the saddle. "I don't like this flower," he whined. "It makes me want to sneeze."

"Rubbish," Simon said. "It's all in the mind."

"Is this horse fast?" Michael asked. "If it isn't, I shall need a big stick."

"That is exactly what you will get if you are not careful," Becky said sourly.

"I hope it is a small class," Simon said. "About ten entries. Then we shall be out of the ring in half an hour."

"Obviously he hasn't seen the catalogue," Mrs. Grey whispered. "There are 67 in the class."

We were horror-struck. "There can't be!" Sarah exclaimed in a low voice. "It's impossible!"

"Oh yes there are," Mrs. Grey said. "There are 67 ponies catalogued. I have seen it with my own eyes," adding to Michael, who was fiddling with the pony's mane, "Don't undo the plaits, dear. They take ages to sew up."

"The preliminary judging is in

the second ring," Becky said. "We had better go and find a space to watch."

"I will just give Michael a trot up and down," Simon said. "Then I will follow you down to the collecting ring."

"If he complains about the flower," Mrs. Grey said, "ignore him. Eventually, he will forget about it."

"If he complains about anything," Simon promised, "I shall throttle him." He led the pony off through a line of horse-boxes and we walked through to the second ring, skirting the deep mud in the gateway, which was the result of heavy rain in the night. Already dozens of little ponies and their attendants were milling about all over the place. The collecting-ring steward was attempting to get them into some sort of order.

Mrs. Grey was aghast. "Surely no Judge can be expected to cope with a class of these proportions?" she said.

"Simon will have a fit when he sees the size of the class," Sarah said.

"I can't wait to see him in the ring," said Becky gleefully. "I have never seen him look such a pansy in my life."

We found a space at the side of the ring as the ponies began to file into the ring, nose to tail. "I wonder how many of the entries are actually forward?" Sarah said. She began to count the ponies.

"I can't see Simon yet," I said.

"Sixteen, seventeen, eighteen,"

Sarah said.

"They ought to be in by now," Mrs. Grey said. "After all, they were all ready when we left them."

"Here they are," Becky said as the grey pony came through from the collecting ring. "No it isn't."

"Twenty-five, twenty-six," Sarah said. "Twenty-seven."

"Of course, they may be already in the ring," Becky said. "In this crowd, we may have missed them."

"Thirty-nine, forty."

"There are such a lot of grey ponies," said Mrs. Grey, squinting across the ring, "and from a distance, they all look alike."

"Fifty-eight, fifty-nine, sixty," Sarah said, adding with satisfaction, "There, I have got back to where I started and Simon is not in the ring."

"Something must have gone wrong," Mrs. Grey decided. We threaded our way back to the collecting ring.

"Is something the matter?" asked the steward, who was clearly at the end of his tether. "If there is, I would rather you did not tell me about it. I am fed up to the back teeth with parents, ponies and small children."

"We know the feeling," Sarah said sympathetically.

"We have lost The Blue Fairy," Becky said. It was a true statement because this happened to be the pony's name.

The steward gave her a suspicious look.

"Of course, it is not exactly blue," Sarah said. "Because it is really grey."

The steward closed his catalogue with a final snap. "I can truthfully say," he said in a voice that implied that we were the absolute end, the final straw, "that I have not seen any fairy. Not today. Not ever." And he walked off.

"He was not exactly helpful," commented Mrs. Grey as we ran along under the tree towards the Exhibitors' Park, which was full of private driving people, winching vehicles out of their boxes and putting together complicated pieces of harness.

"Here's Simon!" Becky cried, and it was. They were just coming out of the nearest line of boxes.

"Where on earth have you been?" we shrieked. "The class has already started!"

"We were all ready to come," Simon said grimly, "when Michael decided he wanted to go to the loo. Then he got his zip stuck. I waited outside the tent for ages. Eventually I had to tie the pony up and go and rescue him. Are we too late? Have we missed the judging?"

"If you are quick, I think you will just make it," Sarah said.

"There are so many ponies in it, it will take ages to see them all. They will never notice a late arrival," Mrs. Grey said. "But do hurry!"

We all raced back towards the collecting ring. We were going through the gateway when somebody shouted, "Mind your backs!" A governess car drove straight through the middle, showering us all with mud. We were all abso-

lutely plastered. The Blue Fairy was spattered all over one side, and as Simon had hastily pulled her aside to get out of the way, Michael had fallen off. He looked as if he had been dipped in chocolate. He was totally covered with mud. We all stood speechless with horror. Michael began to howl.

Simon threw down his cane, ripped off his carnation, hurled his bowler hat as far as he could throw it, and headed for the bar.

We stood abandoned, Becky, Sarah, Mrs. Grey and I. One filthy, howling little boy and a mud bedecked pretty little pony, who stared at us in wonderment out of huge, dark, beautiful eyes.

"Ah well," said Mrs. Grey in resignation. "End of a perfect day."

*A governess car drove straight through the middle, showering us all with mud.*

The wild pony stallions of the Outer Banks, Beaufort, North Carolina, currently have no time to worry about their rivals raiding

# Wild Ponies Of North Carolina

*by Michael Lorant*

their 'harems'. Responsibilities of an even graver nature have settled upon the old warriors, and from atop a dune they sniff the north-west winds of the United States apprehensively. It's 'pony-penning' time, and the older wild horses all know the chaos and confusion which visits their stormy beach when the mainland creatures come in boats, carrying ropes and branding irons.

Early in the morning, the beaters begin driving the ponies down the banks towards the trap, with a line of men which thinly stretches from ocean to sound.

A large number of mainlanders usually attend the penning, as both spectators and participants. When the ponies approach the funnel leading into the pens, these volunteers, armed with leafy twigs, help prevent them passing around the pen, or dashing off into the water.

**The State of North Carolina in the United States is the Eldorado of wild horses that have roamed the outer banks of the State for the last 300 years, ever since a Spanish ship loaded with fine horses was wrecked on this coastline.**

*Top* Ownership of colts is determined by watching whose mares they are following. Here a couple of owners settle who has right to a colt.
*Right* The stallion in the centre of the picture went berserk; he bit and killed one colt and injured other horses before he was cut out of the band and released from the pen.

Once in the pen, owners apply their brands to the colts, identifying them by watching whose mares they are following. Brands are registered in Carteret County courthouse. If any bidders are present, a few may be sold and taken to the mainland, where they are used as pets and riders. Most are turned back upon the lonely dunes to continue the existence they have lived for some 300 years; or ever since, as local tradition has it, a Spanish ship loaded with fine horses was wrecked on this coast.

A wild pony 'penning' is a laborious task. The hardy horses, now dwarfed (450 to 700 pounds), are led by stallions wise to the terrain and its man-made pitfalls, and some of them invariably thunder through the thin line of beaters. The mares and their colts follow the leader unhesitatingly, and even the horse-hunters cannot restrain a cheer when a wise old banker stallion outwits his adversaries. Sometimes he will climb to the top of a sea-oat-tufted dune, and sniff at the danger ahead and behind, while his herd huddles quivering below, the frightened foals nuzzling close to their mares. At this moment a quick decision: the leader sometimes plunges headlong toward the pen, his crowd galloping blindly behind him. But once in a while, he will find a break in the line and, wheeling swiftly, plunge into the sound, reach deep water, and swim round behind the discouraged beaters.

At one time, all the Outer Banks of North Carolina contained ponies, but now they are confined mostly to Ocracoke Island and to Shackleford and Core Banks. They have a precarious existence, subsisting on coarse beach vegetation, and often pawing shallow wells for drink. When the brackish water seeps up, they will lie on their bellies to get to it.

Once they were so numerous that they would swim across the sound to the mainland, where they were said to race wildly up and down the hard oyster roads, making such a clatter as to disturb Sabbath worship.

Originally ownerless, the ponies gradually were rounded up and branded and became private property, though they range without hindrance along the beaches. On Ocracoke Island, most of the ponies belong to Stanly Wahab,

**A colt is branded while other horses look on. The mare to the left of the picture is calling to a stallion.**

sixth descendant of Ahab Wahab, an Arab sailor shipwrecked on the island in the 18th century. Wahab, now a well-to-do Baltimore man, loosed a thoroughbred polo pony stallion on the island and greatly improved the breed there.

While the ponies have little economic value, they require no attention, and seem to be considered as family heirlooms on the Banks.

That the ponies are masters of their maritime environment is not disputed locally. It is said that a few years ago a Carteret County man, who made a hobby of training the ponies, bought a young one at the Ocracoke penning and brought him to the mainland. One night, the beast escaped and was not seen again until his owner revisited the island. There he saw his duly-branded horse happily back on his wind-swept sandbar. To get there, the pony had performed an almost incredible feat—he had waded and swum six miles to Shackleford Bank, and after a long walk had crossed Barden Inlet; then, after rounding Cape Lookout, had travelled up lonely Core Banks, and plunged into Drum Inlet. From there he followed the beach to Portsmouth and finally breasted the dangerous currents of Ocracoke Inlet—a journey which might have upset even a well-equipped safari.

# Spring . . .

*"You were the one who said it was time to start Spring cleaning!"*

# Wild Cherry

**by Elizabeth Hawthorne**

**Illustrated by Ellen Gilbert**

Every morning I used to get out of bed and go to the window, and look longingly at the paddock across the road. It stood, empty and waiting; and I had full permission from the farmer to put my pony in it. The problem was, I had no pony. The money-box on my window-sill was quite full, but not full enough to buy Cherry.

She was for sale. She came to the

riding stable where I rode at the end of the Easter holidays, and I fell in love with her immediately. She was a beautiful, dainty bay mare with the sweetest nature I have ever known. She was a lovely, willing ride, and she was one of the county's foremost junior jumping ponies.

When I went to the riding stables I always went straight to her box to see her. Wild Cherry, the best pony in the world. She would come over to the door and gently breathe into my hand and nuzzle me with her black-tipped nose.

One day as I patted her firm brown neck and straightened her long black mane, Kathy, the stable girl, came over to me and leaned on her broom, looking Cherry over.

"There are two people coming to see her tomorrow," she said finally.

My heart sank. It was inevitable; everyone knew Cherry's reputation and only the high asking price had prevented her from being sold already. I had lain awake for several nights wondering how to raise more money, but the price was far above my small savings.

"Who are they?" I asked anxiously, hoping it was someone I knew.

"Mary Thorn, and," Kathy paused before she added, "the Benders."

I knew both names. Mary Thorn had ridden at the stables. She was a nice gentle girl, and though not very experienced would probably do well with Cherry. But the Benders . . .

"Not the Benders!" I groaned.

"Cherry couldn't go with Snooker, he looks like a donkey!"

Kathy laughed. "He's a very successful pony, nonetheless," she reminded me. "However, I hope Mary buys Cherry; she would give her a good home."

We were all against the Benders at the riding stables. The twin girls, Pamela and Sally, were nice enough, I suppose, but they were terribly competitive in the worst sort of way. They gloated when they won, and complained when they lost. I think their father drove them to it; he always chased Snooker over the practice jump at shows with a lot of shouting and arm-waving. He had bought several ponies and sold them again before finding Snooker, who was a consistent winner, and Cherry was an obvious choice to make up a pair.

"We'll make sure that Mary buys you," I promised Cherry, who flicked her ears and showed no sign of worry about her future.

The following day was spent in preparing for the new school term, but I finally visited the stables in the afternoon. Cherry was still in her box, but it was some time before I could drag Kathy away from her various duties to tell me what had happened.

"The Thorns want her," Kathy told me. I could have yelled my relief. "They're just waiting for a vet's certificate before they take her."

"I am glad," I said. Actually I felt very sad at the thought of Cherry leaving, but I knew she was going to a kind home. "What did the Benders say?" I asked.

"They were furious," laughed Kathy. "They offered a higher price, but we had already promised her to the Thorns. They said to be sure to let them know if the Thorns changed their mind."

Since Cherry had been waiting in her box all day to be seen, she needed exercise, and Kathy let me take her out. She was a heavenly ride, and she stepped out eagerly along the grass verge. It was a lovely mild spring evening, and I made the most of it because I thought it would probably be the last time Cherry and I were together.

I took her through the woods and out onto the bridle path. She was longing for a canter, so I let her go. As we thundered up the path I imagined she was mine, and that we had won thousands of rosettes together and were the world champion junior show jumpers. When I pulled her up and

*. . . she was a heavenly ride . . .*

turned back to the stable I imagined I was taking her home to the paddock across the road. Her firm brown ears flicked back towards me as I talked to her, and I patted her warm strong neck and let the reins loose as we ambled home.

School started the next day. I don't know how I got through the lessons, and then there was homework. When I reached the stables, all my waiting had been in vain, for the vet had not come. The following evening, however, I could tell from Kathy's face that something had happened.

"The vet's been?" I guessed.

She nodded. I looked at her uneasily. Why wasn't she telling me cheerily that Mary was going to take Cherry, and all was well? Instead she turned away from me and led the way to Cherry's box. We stood looking at her for a few moments, and at last Kathy said, "She's unsound."

I looked at the pony before me. She was the picture of health; her eyes were bright and her bay coat glowed. There couldn't be anything wrong with her.

"I don't believe it," I said dully.

"It's her legs," Kathy said. "Her forelegs are weak. The vet said she needs a year's rest."

I stood stupidly, looking at the large dark eyes of the pony nuzzling at the pocket of my jacket. Kathy didn't say any more, and we just stood there until I finally said, "I suppose Mary won't buy her and rest her?" Kathy shook her head. "She wanted to, but her parents pointed out that she's

growing so fast that Cherry would be too small in a year or so. And Cherry isn't getting any younger, either."

I turned away from the box. Through my gloom a tiny hope was wavering. I wouldn't outgrow Cherry in a year. Would her unsoundness push the price down to my level?

"We haven't told the Benders yet," Kathy interrupted my thoughts. "They might still be interested."

The little hope rocketed out of reach. I suddenly felt hard and cold.

"They won't be put off by a little unsoundness," I said angrily. "They'll jump her till she drops!"

Wild Cherry was sold the following day to Mr. Bender. I stayed away from the stables the day she left, and it seemed so empty afterwards without her. The weeks wore on and we heard nothing about her, and I began to think that perhaps I had wronged the Benders, and that they were resting her after all.

The summer holidays arrived, and the shows and gymkhanas began in earnest. At the first gymkhana I went to I rode a young pony called Flash. I was walking him around away from the crowd when Pat, one of the younger girls from the stables, came bouncing towards me on fat old Dolly.

"Cherry's here!" she yelled at me. "They've hogged her mane!"

I felt happiness, anger and sorrow in quick succession as I thought of seeing Cherry, then of her beautiful mane, and then her weak legs. Poor old Cherry.

Pat told me that she had seen her in the collecting ring, waiting her turn in the jumping. Snooker had apparently jumped a clear round.

I rode over to the ring and halted Flash opposite the collecting ring. I could pick out Cherry a mile away, in spite of her short mane. She looked well, but I saw with horror that she was wearing a heavy Pelham bit and a martingale.

"Why have they done that?" I almost shouted at Pat, who didn't understand my fury. "Cherry has a perfect mouth!"

I saw Snooker standing nearby, and understood the reason. The two bay ponies were the same height, and he had a hogged mane, Pelham and martingale. Twin ponies for twin girls.

Sally was riding Cherry into the ring. I couldn't help but wish the gallant pony would win.

"Sally Bender on Pin Ball," came the announcer's voice.

Pin Ball, to go with Snooker. The final blow. I must confess that I fought back tears while I watched my lovely Wild Cherry jumping like a stag. She was right on form and won easily.

After that we saw Cherry regularly at the shows. At first she won constantly, but I began to notice the strain which her forelegs were under as she jumped. Her legs seemed to bend right back at the knee every time she landed, and she began to stumble

frequently. At one show I found myself standing and talking with a group of riders who included Pamela Bender. She was sitting on Cherry, and I suppose what initially annoyed me was that Pamela was quite a lot fatter than Sally, and I wished that Cherry didn't have to carry the extra weight. Then I heard her calling Cherry 'Cheery'. It was better than Pin Ball, but it encouraged me to say to Pamela rather suddenly, "How are Cherry's legs?"

Pamela looked a bit uncomfortable, and a girl I didn't know asked, "What's wrong with them?"

Pamela didn't say anything, and since everyone was looking at me I said, "She has weak forelegs. I thought she had to be rested."

"Oh, that," Pamela mumbled, staring rather hard into Cherry's mane.

I felt mean then. I could imagine Mr. Bender refusing to rest Cherry and the girls being unhappy about it but not daring to fight back. Everyone was looking at Pamela rather balefully, waiting for an explanation. I tried to save the situation by saying, "She looks well."

About half-way through the summer Cherry stopped coming to the shows. No one seemed to know what had happened to her, and I did not dare ask Pamela or Sally, after the scene I had made. I was standing by the ring one day watching Snooker jump, when I heard voices behind me.

"Did those new shoes do any good to your other pony?"

*. . . she never faltered, she faced each jump bravely and flew over it.*

"No. Lame as ever. We're trying another pair."

I did not have to look to know it was Mr. Bender. I stiffened with anger when I realised that he was forcing Cherry to keep going.

"She must be ready for the Melworth Show," Mr. Bender was saying, then he moved away to congratulate Pamela on her clear round.

Ready or not, Cherry was at the Melworth Show. It was one of the biggest local shows, held in September, and the riding school turned out in force for the last show before school started. I was riding Flash again, and the first pony I saw was Cherry. She looked as well as ever. Her ears were pricked as she walked calmly around the showground with her long, steady stride, without a trace of lameness. Her front legs were bandaged, which was common

enough for jumping ponies, but when Sally saw me looking at them she blushed and turned away.

I rode Flash in the novice jumping. He was a nice little jumper, and I was pleased to get him round the course with only four faults, for as always at Melworth the jumps were high. I put him away and settled myself by the ringside to see Cherry in the junior jumping.

She jumped clear, and as I watched I remembered the phrase, 'ride a willing horse to death'. Every jump must have been painful to her, for the strain on landing and the stumbling were more obvious than ever. But she never faltered; she faced each jump bravely and flew over it. Her coat was dark with sweat when she cantered out of the ring.

As I watched the fences going up

for the jump-off, I began to feel desperate. What could I do? I wondered if I should report the Benders to the show authorities. I sat by the ringside in indecision, and was still sitting there when Cherry came in to jump again.

The jumps were high, for the standard was high. Cherry jumped as usual, but on landing after the wall she pecked badly. The crowd gasped, for it looked as if she was going to fall, but she collected herself and cantered on to the last jump. She cantered lame.

A buzz of excitement arose from the crowd as they saw what was happening. Sally made no effort to pull up, but sat there as if she didn't know what to do. I saw the tremendous effort which Cherry made to get over that jump. Get over it she did, and it was her last jump. Her legs gave way on landing. She turned a complete somersault and lay still.

I leapt to my feet and stood looking at the inert brown body. Sally had been thrown clear and was sitting up, looking dazed. People were running into the ring. Someone helped Sally to her feet and led her away. Mr. Bender was at Cherry's head, looking at her, and suddenly he pulled at the reins. Cherry got to her feet.

I came back to reality as I saw that Cherry wasn't dead, but was being led hobbling out of the ring. I ran after her.

The vet was there, examining her legs, and talking to Mr. Bender.

"Looks as though the ligament's ruptured," I heard him say. "You'll have to have her put down, unless you want to breed from her."

"She'll only pass on the unsoundness," said Mr. Bender gloomily. "Not necessarily," the vet said. "It depends on whether this weakness is in the conformation or caused by overwork."

"I'd rather collect the slaughterer's price than take the chance," Mr. Bender said.

I was turning hot and cold with horror and anger. I hardly knew what I was doing, but I found myself tugging at his sleeve and saying, "I'll give you the slaughterer's price for her."

I didn't even know what that was, but I knew that if I didn't have it in my money-box I would raise it somehow.

Mr. Bender hardly looked at me, but said, "Collect her tomorrow, then."

He led Cherry away and left me standing there, my head whirling with excitement and nerves as I realised what I was doing.

Now when I get up in the morning I don't wait to look out of the window. I go straight over to the paddock, and Wild Cherry comes over to me, limping slightly but looking fat and happy. She searches my hands gently for anything I might bring her, and her son tickles my arm with his whiskers in his curiosity. I took the chance, and I know that when he grows up he is going to be the best junior jumping pony in the country.

**H.R.H. PRINCESS ANNE.** This happy picture of Princess Anne, the 1971 European Horse Trials Champion, was taken in the rain at Hickstead in July 1973, when she was competing there for the first time and won the Combined Open Championship on Doublet. At the Badminton Horse Trials this year she finished fourth on Goodwill.

# Famous Faces *Photographed by Sheila Hughes*

**RICHARD MEADE.** This informal portrait study of Britain's 'Golden Boy of Eventing' was taken at Hickstead in April 1973, the year after he won the individual gold medal at the Munich Olympics on Major Derek Allhusen's Laurieston.

**ANN BACKHOUSE.** A former Ladies' European Champion, Ann Backhouse has gone a long way on Cardinal since she won the European Junior Show Jumping Championship on Irish Lace in 1958 at the age of 18.

34

**ANN MOORE** has written herself into the annals of show-jumping history with her achievements on Psalm, the horse on whom she won two Ladies' European Championships and the silver medal at the Munich Olympics.
**CAROLINE BRADLEY,** one of Britain's most elegant show-jumping riders, pictured at Windsor in May 1973.

...Summer

# Early Riding Lessons

**Explained by**
**Jane M. Strachan**

You will often hear of a riding instructor talking about the importance of the 'balanced' seat as this is the first basic essential necessary for riding well. It is, in effect, the safest and easiest method of sitting on a pony and, what is even more important, it allows the animal freedom and comfort whilst being ridden. We can divide the rider's position in the saddle into four: seat, back, legs and hands, and when these are all understood they can be put together to work in accordance with each other and obtain the necessary results.

**Seat.**

The key to remember here is the 'three-point contact' which is formed by the two seat bones and the crutch. If you are sitting too far back in the saddle the contact of the crutch will be unequal to that of the seat bones; and similarly, if you sit too far forward, the two seat bones will have an uneven contact with the saddle. This 'three-point contact' is most important, as you will not be able to use your legs, back and hands properly until you are sitting correctly. It should follow that you will be sitting in the deepest part of the saddle where stillness and balance are the all-important factors.

**Back.**

It is a very common fault to disregard the back as an aid; it is, in fact, as important as your legs and hands. The bracing and relaxing of the back plays a major part in the increasing and decreasing of speed. The back should, of course, be kept straight at all times; nothing looks worse than a rider slouching in the saddle, and the muscles will perform the activities of bracing and relaxing. When your back is braced and your seat well down in the saddle working in conjunction with legs and hands, the pony will slow down, whilst with the back relaxed in conjunction with the other aids the pony should increase his pace.

**Legs.**

Many people have difficulty in keeping their legs in the right position but this should not be a problem if you are sitting correctly to begin with. As a rough guide, there should be a straight line from the shoulder to the elbow to the hip to the heel, with the knees resting against the saddle and the lower leg hanging still and naturally against the pony's sides. The toes should always be pointing forwards and the heels kept down.

With your lower leg in the right position, just behind the girth, and resting against the pony's sides, you will find that the aids for increasing and decreasing speed require little movement of the legs. If you have ever watched skilled riders carefully you will have noticed that it is difficult to detect any movement at all in the leg when aids are given, and this is what you should aim for. When the lower leg is used to slow down, do not use your heels but just close your legs against the pony's sides. This will push up his quarters, and keep him on the bit and well balanced. Your legs are also used in this way to ask the pony to lengthen his stride in any pace.

**Hands**

The upper part of your arm, from your shoulder to your elbow, should always be kept against your sides, hence the familiar cry "elbows in". Then from your elbow through your wrists (which should be kept flexible) to your hands and then along the reins to the pony's mouth there should be a straight line. Your hands should always be about four inches apart, which is approximately the same width as the pony's mouth, and they should be about two inches in front of the pommel of the saddle. The reins should lie along the base of your fingers, passing between the little finger and the fourth finger, with your thumbs on the top and finger-nails of both hands facing each other.

It is often said that to have

good hands is a gift, or something that you are born with, and it is true that many children seem to have a natural 'feel' for the pony's mouth. However, there are certain points that must be remembered by everyone in connection with their hands; a pony's tongue and the bars of his mouth on which the bit rests are extremely sensitive, as under the thin layer of skin is a complicated network of tiny nerves that register the slightest pressure in the pony's brain. This is why the hands must always be kept still and sympathetic whilst maintaining even contact. It is a good idea to imagine that you are holding a thread of cotton instead of a leather rein. This should give you an idea of how delicately your pony's mouth should be handled.

## Understanding the Problems.

Bad riding accounts for a great many of the faults that develop in ponies and the longer these faults are allowed to continue the more difficult it will be to correct them. In older ponies it may even be impossible to re-educate if the faults have gone unchecked for several years.

Faulty distribution of weight is the cause of many problems and, since all horses are at an initial disadvantage because the normal weight of their head and neck is disproportionate to the rest of the body, your pony must learn to balance himself naturally with the added weight of the rider. However, bad conformation can also be the reason why a horse does not carry himself well, and this generally affects the position of his head and the distribution of his own weight.

Ponies with short, thick necks may find it difficult to stretch their necks and flex sufficiently at the poll, but the poll must always be the highest point of the horse's head, regardless of conformation. Preliminary schooling forms the basis of how every pony balances itself and learns to cope with the rider's weight, so we can sometimes blame bad breaking and schooling for a pony's faults. It is not uncommon to find a pony leaning heavily on the bit, and he does this to seek support from the bit if too much weight is being carried on the forehand either through bad schooling or a bad rider.

A horse that is broken too quickly and does not have time to accustom itself to carrying a rider's weight with the necessary lowered head and arched back may do the reverse and hold its head too high in order to alleviate the rider's weight. If a pony constantly carries its head too high, and its back is unnaturally low, it can develop a weak back and will consequently be unable to perform as well as a normal pony.

Very often the root of the trouble lies in the horse's mouth and is directly linked to the rider's hands. You will probably have heard a horse being described as 'hard mouthed' and this means that owing either to an ill-fitting or severe bit or to a heavy-handed rider, or both, the tiny nerves (mentioned above) have been dam- aged, so that the horse no longer feels a normal contact with the bit. Many animals will put their heads up to evade the harsh action of the bit but by so doing they transfer the action of the bit from the bars of the mouth to the lips, which are even more sensitive and therefore liable to cause the horse even greater pain. A horse may also resort to snatching at the reins, yawing or even bolting to relieve the pressure on his mouth for a brief moment, and for this the rider alone is to blame.

A pony that has got into the habit of evading the bit, or carrying his head too high for any other reason, can be corrected in time by the use of a very mild bit and a good rider who will encourage him to lower his head not by pressure on the reins but by using the seat and legs to push the quarters up to make him accept the bit.

There are, of course, a great many problems that beset the young horse and rider, and whilst some can be remedied by the rider himself it is often best to seek the help of an experienced person who may be able to detect faults that you may not have realised are there. One last point to remember is that although a pony is sometimes at fault this can nearly always be traced back to poor handling at some time in his life; and unless you are convinced that your riding is perfect, you can safely assume that it is you who must improve before you can expect any improvement from your pony.

41

# Home Run

*by Bess Leese*

**Illustrated by Nicola Beckett**

"You are the guest," said Josie. "You choose where to go."

Which was silly, really, because Penny had never stayed with her cousin before, and did not know the country at all.

"Well, we could ride along the sea wall," said Josie. "Only Crystal gets very excited along the sea wall, and you might fall off. Or we could go across the stubble fields to the farm, only the bicycle might get a puncture." (They were sharing a pony and a bicycle between them.) "Or we could go to Fox Hill Woods, which are super, only you have to cross the main road."

If Crystal had been asked for his choice, he would have said without hesitation, "Fox Hill Woods," because on the way to the Woods, just after you had crossed the main road, was J. A. Parkin's General Stores. Nobody, least of all Josie, passed J. A. Parkin's General Stores without stopping to buy chocolate or mint imperials or Pontefract cakes. Crystal liked all those sweets, in that order of preference. However, nobody consulted him because he was only a pony and could not speak.

"Will Crystal mind the traffic on the main road?" Penny asked.

"Of course not," said Josie. "It's just that if you fall off he won't wait for you, he'll run home, and if nobody catches him he might run into a lorry or something."

"I won't fall off," said Penny, but Josie seemed unconvinced.

"Crystal's not a riding-school slug," she pointed out. "He has a lot of quality."

Penny knew that she was quoting her private instructor, and she felt compelled to say, "Not all riding-school ponies are slugs. Lots of them are very nice." Which was the most she dared say without actually being rude to Josie.

But she had to admit that Crystal was a lovely animal, and he was certainly different from any school pony she had ever sat on. Full of beans and bus-tickets, as her riding-mistress would have said. He suspected everything. He knew that there was something nasty lurking round every corner. He knew that at any minute a bogeyman would spring out at him from behind the hedge. He knew that some hidden terror lay inside the paper bag blowing down the lane, and he was not on any account going to go past that heap of sand, which had certainly not been there last week, until Josie had been past it first on the bicycle. He was an interesting ride.

It was true that he didn't mind traffic, but he fidgeted like an irksome child at the main road while they waited for a chance to cross. It was an awful road, a dual carriageway, and Penny saw why Josie had misgivings about it. But Crystal did not care tuppence about the cars and containers, the tankers and transporters and great articulated lorries that thundered past under his nose.

*. . . he fidgeted like an irksome child while they waited for a chance to cross the road.*

His mind was definitely on chocolate, peppermints and Pontefract cakes from J. A. Parkin's General Stores.

"We'll swap over at the shop," said Josie. "You can have the bicycle."

She bought a disgustingly large quantity of chocolate and sweets at the Stores, and Penny wished that she was not a guest but merely a friend, so that she could be rude and say, "No wonder you are too fat." But Josie shared out the sweets equally between herself, Crystal and Penny; and Crystal had a carrot as well which he helped himself to out of a wooden box standing on the bench outside the shop.

"We had better go," said Penny, "before Mr. J. A. Parkin notices the carrot."

"He can't notice it now," Josie pointed out. "It's gone."

*. . . still in the saddle was Josie, her jeans and white T-shirt immaculate . . .*

She sat casually in the saddle, reins dangling, her feet out of the stirrups half the time, while Crystal snorted and shied all the way to Fox Hill Woods.

"What he wants is a really good gallop," she said, and as she thundered off into the blue distance down a grassy bridle track, Penny knew that she was showing off again. Of course, Josie was a better rider. If you rode every day, and had private instruction into the bargain, you were bound to be better than somebody who only had one hour's lesson once a week. Penny had already suffered a cross-examination which consisted of questions like, "Don't you jump anything except cavalletti?" and "Do you mean to say you can't do a turn on the forehand?" And she was beginning to wish that something mildly unpleasant would happen to Josie. A minor humiliation like being bucked off into a bed of nettles or a muddy pool would do.

It was too much to hope for. Penny pedalled uncomfortably down the bridle track; and there, waiting by a little wicket gate, still in the saddle, was Josie, her jeans and white T-shirt immaculate, no tell-tale signs of grass stains, no rash of nettle stings on her arms and face.

"You can have a gallop now," she said. "Once we get through the gate you can't come to any harm. It won't matter if you fall off because Crystal can't get out of the woods here."

"I shan't fall off," said Penny,

though she wasn't quite confident that this was true. One good gallop was not enough to quieten Crystal down. In fact, it seemed to have primed him for further adventures, and before Penny had even gathered the reins he set off through the woods as though the Devil were on his tail. Startled rabbits scuttled into the bushes. A pheasant ran shrieking out of his path, and in the treetops the pigeons' wings cracked like gunshots as they took to the sky.

"I will not fall off," thought Penny, fishing desperately for a lost stirrup. She shortened up the reins and, with both feet secure in the irons again, she was safe. She spoke to Crystal and gently checked him. He gave one buck, his last joyful fling, and then finding she was still in the saddle, settled down to a steady, long-striding canter.

It was bliss, especially because Josie was miles away by the wicket gate where she could not see what Penny was doing. So after a while, Penny took Crystal off the bridle track and found some logs to jump, and some fallen branches with twigs that stuck up like a bullfinch, and a little ditch where she lost her stirrups again.

"You've been ages," Josie complained. "I thought you'd fallen off."

"I hardly ever fall off," said Penny, taking over the bicycle.

It was Josie who fell off. She fell off going through the wicket gate. Neither of them knew precisely how it happened. Somehow, as Josie drew her leg up to avoid banging it on the gatepost, the saddleflap got caught up, and then the latch impaled itself in the girth buckles. Immediately Crystal panicked. He could neither go backwards nor forwards. The latch dug into his ribs. He bucked and plunged and kicked out at Penny behind. The girth burst apart. The saddle and Josie, and Josie's hard hat, which had parted company with her head just when it was most needed, hurtled to the ground. Crystal was free.

"Catch him!" screamed Josie, battling with the saddle, which was sitting squarely on her chest. "Quick! Before he gets to the main road."

There was no time to lose. Penny wheeled the bicycle over Josie's foot and set off in pursuit. Her legs pumped the pedals round and round, her face went purple with

*The saddle and Josie, and Josie's hard hat, hurtled to the ground.*

effort. Yet what was the good? Crystal moved with the speed of light. The last she saw of him was the flick of his silvery tail as he disappeared round a bend. A cloud of dust settled in his wake.

She hoped somebody would stop him. Some hero, surely, would stand in his path, arms out-stretched, saying "Whoa, whoa boy," like they did in books.

Somebody did. "I tried to stop your pony," said an old man who had been cleaning the ditches, "but he nearly knocked me over. You want to catch him before he gets to the main road, else there'll be a nasty accident."

Penny pedalled on. It was all up to her, yet she knew she couldn't catch him. What chance had a mere bicycle against Crystal? He was built for speed. Uphill, down-hill, it was all one to him. To Penny, her breath raw in her lungs, it seemed mostly grindingly uphill. "He's going that way," people said as she puffed by; but she did not need telling. She knew exactly which way he was going. He was going home. Nobody had taught him to look right, left, then right again. He was going across the dual carriageway, right in the teeth of the coastbound traffic, the lorries, the containers, the rattling car-transporters. Thirty tons of steel would see the end of Crystal.

Penny cried as she pedalled, and the tears coursed down her beet-root cheeks and turned to vapour on her parched lips. She cried all the way to J. A. Parkin's General Stores. And then she stopped.

For there was Mr. J. A. Parkin himself, standing outside his shop. In his hand he held a Pontefract cake, and nosing at the Pontefract cake, as calm and untroubled as a summer's day, was Crystal.

"Isn't this that fat little girl's pony?" said Mr. J. A. Parkin.

"My cousin's, yes," gasped Penny. "Thank you very much for catching him."

"Didn't do a thing," said Mr. J. A. Parkin. "Just saw him wait-ing here. Stopped off for a bag of toffees, I reckon. He's a regular customer. Are you all right, both of you?"

"Yes, thank you," said Penny. She hadn't spared a thought for Josie, but she knew she must be all right by the way she had screamed orders. "I'll ride Crystal back."

"Bareback?" said Mr. J. A. Parkin admiringly. "You won't fall off?"

"No," said Penny. "Not me."

"I'll give you a leg up then. You can leave your bike by the fence."

Penny thanked him yet again.

"Don't mention it," said Mr. J. A. Parkin, seeing her off. And he turned back to his customers.

"A pound of carrots, did you say? Certainly, my dear." And then he scratched his head. "I could have sworn . . ." he said, puzzled. "I haven't sold a carrot all day."

But there was no denying that the carrot box on the bench out-side his shop was empty. Absolute-ly empty.

# Crossword Puzzle

## Compiled by Jeannelle Dening-Smitherman

**Answers on page 88**

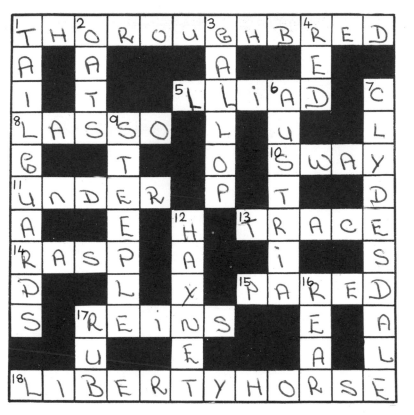

### Clues Across

1. Horse of pure breed. (12)
5. Wooden Horse of Troy appears in this epic poem by Homer. (5)
8. Noosed rope used by cowboys. (5)
10. _____-backed; horse with abnormally hollowed back. (4)
11. _____-reach; in trotting, the toe of the fore-shoe scrapes the hind toe. (5)
13. One of the side straps in harness. (5)
14. Long-handled file used by farriers. (4)
15. Hooves are clipped or _____ (5)
17. The hands, through these, are aids. (5)
18. Circus horse which performs unridden. (12)

### Clues Down

1. Made of rugging or leather to prevent damage when travelling. (10)
2. Preferably crushed or rolled. (4)
3. A fast pace of four time. (6)
4. _____ ribbon indicates a kicker. (3)
6. Country of origin of the Lipizzaner. (7)
7. Breed native to Lanarkshire, Scotland. (10)
9. _____ chase, a race with obstacles of fences, ditches and water. (7)
12. Corded receptacle for dried grass. (6)
16. Rise on hind feet. (4)
17. _____-down; given to a sweating or wet horse. (3)

47

# Definition Of A Horse

*by Ann Douglas*

**A**cceleration is horses playing in the paddock.

**B**eauty is when something catches your horse's eye, and he stares transfixed, and you stare mesmerized by the density of his beauty.

**C**haracter is contained in every horse.

**D**efiance is the playful buck on a cold winter's morning.

**E**agerness is a taut rein on a fit horse.

**F**leabitten is freckles on a grey horse as he gets old.

**G**ait is when a young horse learns to collect for the first time.

**H**armony is the soft thud of a horse's hooves on green turf when serenaded by the song of the birds.

**I**dentification is when a horse neighs to a long-lost friend.

**J**ealousy is choosing a pile of hay at feeding time.

**K**indness is moving over when another horse wants to drink at the trough as well.

**L**ove is a horse walking to the gate when you want to catch him.

**M**elancholy moments are such as when a tired horse wanders off when turned out at the end of a hot day.

**N**eighing is an expression of love, friendship, and happiness.

**O**dour is the smell of clean tack, wet horse, and new hay.

**P**eace is the end of the day when all the horses are knee-deep in fresh clean straw, when their rugs are square and cover large clean quarters, when their noses are buried in a feed bucket, when there is a bulging haynet filled with clean sweet hay at the back of the stable.

**Q**uivering is when a young horse has a new experience.

48

**R**eflex actions are when you say thank you to a horse who moves over unasked.

**S**everity is when after turning out a horse he stands expectantly until you have expressed your love and respect by the gentle rubbing of his nose.

**T**ranquillity is grazing a horse in a green field.

**U**nbridled is the action of a free horse.

**V**aliant is the horse which passes a fluttering paper bag.

**W**agons are the reminder of a past rich with horses.

**X**-Rays are the factors which determine between the life or death of a friend.

**Y**ards are the central show piece or a heaven for horses.

**Z**ebras are a reminder that even people in distant parts have the joy of the equine animal.

---

## Autumn . . .

*"I can never understand why the opening meet brings out all your primitive instincts."*

50

Routine is a very important aspect in the care of a stable-kept pony. This is because a pony is a creature of habit and therefore likes to be fed, groomed and exercised at the same time each day. Once in a while a complete routine is not possible owing to an outing or visit to a show but on the whole the same daily schedule should be strictly maintained. There is, however, one very important point that I should like to make and this is that anyone undertaking to keep a pony in a stable must make sure that the animal is fed regularly. If you cannot do this yourself get a reliable friend to do it.

To demonstrate how important it is to keep your pony's feed times regular, put yourself in his place. You have been standing in your box all morning and the built-in clock in your stomach starts telling you that it is nearly time for your mid-day feed. You watch eagerly over your stable door for your owner to appear carrying your feed bowl. Saliva slowly trickles into your mouth in anticipation and your ears prick to try to catch the sound of creaking corn bins. With impatience you start to bang the door with your knees. A few seconds later you are sharply rebuked by your owner who appears from the feed room with your bowl in her hands. Obediently you stand over to one side as she tips the feed into the manger, knowing that no pushing will be tolerated. At last she moves out of the way and happily you start to tuck in.

That is the happy story of a pony whose owner keeps to a strict feeding timetable. It can, however, be very different: Again it is time for your mid-day feed and all the signs of anticipation appear. But time goes by and there is no sign of activity near the feed room. You start to feel irritable and work off your anger by gnawing at the woodwork of your stable or by 'stomping' round and round your box. An hour or so later your owner arrives with your feed, but you no longer feel hungry and you greet her with flattened ears and wrinkled nostrils.

Obviously a pony treated in the latter fashion will become irritable and unhappy. His digestion will become impaired and so his health will suffer. It is clear that a happy pony in the stable will be a more

# Daily Routine For The Stable-Kept Pony

*by Veronica Riches B.H.S.A.I.*

relaxed and cheerful ride than a pony that is irritable and jumpy through bad stable management. Our aim, therefore, must be to make our ponies enjoy our company as we go about the daily routine, and ensure that they have fixed hours each day, during which they can rest undisturbed. This last point is particularly important when there are young children around, who if left to themselves are likely to fuss around the ponies all day.

The following routine is the one I have found best for my young pony Skibbereen.

**7.00 a.m.**
—I go into Skibbereen's stable, remove his rug which has slipped slightly during the night, and lay it over the door. I then stand back and give him a quick look over to check there is nothing amiss, such as a filled leg or a runny nose. Satisfied, I quickly replace the rug before he starts to feel cold.

Next I refill the water bucket so that he has a chance to drink before I muck out. I remove the haynet and refill it. If there is any hay left in the haynet I take it out and put it in a pile ready for the field ponies. It is important that a pony should be given his morning haynet at least half an hour before his first feed; munching the hay helps to start the digestive juices working and also, as hay is digested quicker than concentrates, if eaten after the feed it will push the concentrates out of the stomach before they have been properly digested.

After hanging the haynet up in the stable, I collect a head-collar from the tack room and my mucking-out tools from the barn and get down to the job of mucking out. I always tie my pony up with a piece of string which is tied onto the ring in the stable wall. This I find saves many minor accidents: if the pony takes fright and pulls back sharply, the string will break, whereas had he been tied directly to the ring in the wall he would most likely panic and injure himself or break the headcollar.

When I have piled up all the clean straw in the corner of the box and put the dirty straw in the barrow, I sweep the floor and then clean out Skibbereen's feet into a skip, checking also that his shoes are in order. The feet should be cleaned out at least three times a day because if manure is allowed to remain in them it may cause a disease known as thrush. Next I put down the clean straw, shaking it up well to make a comfortable springy bed, and if necessary collect some new straw from the barn. I then empty the water bucket, scrub it out and refill it.

**8.30 a.m.**
—Skibbereen gets his morning feed.

**9.30 a.m.**
—I collect a headcollar, grooming kit, skip and fork. If it is a warm day I like to groom my pony out in the yard as I am sure he enjoys the sun on his back, and in this way the dust and grease from his coat does not circulate in the open air as it does in the box.

While Skibbereen is standing tied up, I skip up any droppings in his box and tidy the straw with a fork, ready for when he returns from exercise. Then I give him a quick brush over, brush out the straw from his tail, wipe his eyes, nose and dock with damp sponges and check that there is no manure in his feet. I always apply hoof oil to his feet before setting off on exercise as it helps to keep the feet healthy and also improves their appearance. After tacking up Skibbereen I give his rug a good shake and hang it inside-out over the gate to air.

If it is a cold day, while grooming I leave the rug lying over my pony's back, folding it over as I brush the different parts of his body.

**10.00 a.m.**

—1½ to 2 hours' exercise.

It is a good idea, if the fields are not too wet, to school your pony for a few minutes before you set off on a ride. This way he will not become strained or bored by too much schooling all at one time, and if you start your hack after he has performed some movement well will tend to regard the ride as a reward.

**12.00 hrs.**

—On returning from my ride I lead Skibbereen into the stable, remove his tack and throw the rug over his back.

I try to bring him home from exercise in a comfortable condition, i.e., if it is a hot day I will loosen the girth and walk the last mile or so home, but if the day is crisp I will trot on the way back so as to

Headcollar rope tied to string for safety. Below *A quick release knot.*

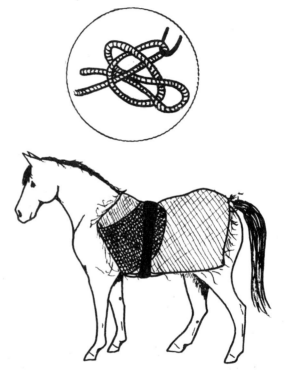

Pony 'thatched' to dry off. Note the rug turned back under surcingle.

bring him in warm but not sweaty.

If it has been raining and Skibbereen is wet, I throw the rug over him inside-out, stuff some straw underneath the rug and put on his roller. The straw traps air underneath the rug, providing insulation which allows the coat to dry. Then I give him a titbit, check for stones in his feet, top up his water and leave him to eat his hay.

One should try to arrange the pony's exercise so that he comes back to his stable at least half an hour before his mid-day feed; otherwise he will be so intent upon the arrival of his feed that he will not have a drink until after he has eaten, and, as you know, this may cause colic.

**1.00 p.m.**
—Skip up droppings. Renew water. Feed.

Water standing in a stable absorbs some of the odours and acidity from the air; therefore stale water should be thrown away and replaced by fresh water two or three times a day.

**3.00 pm.**
—Back to the stables. I skip up any droppings, top up the water and tidy the straw. I next scrub out the manger as any bran left in the bottom will go sour and spoil the next feed.

After that I tie Skibbereen to the piece of string, remove his rug and give him a thorough grooming lasting about half an hour. If it is a dry day I lead him out to have ten minutes' graze, as a little grass each day does a stabled pony the world of good.

With Skibbereen back in his box I get on with some of the extra jobs that tend to build up.

**6.00 p.m.**
—Clean tack.

**7.00 p.m.**
—Adjust Skibbereen's rug. Even

if the rug does not appear to have slipped, it should be adjusted regularly as it will tend to become tight over the withers and shoulders.

Skip up the droppings, renew the water and refill the haynet.

**7.30 p.m.**
—Feed.

**8.30 p.m.**
—Skip up droppings. I find it best to leave Skibbereen two buckets of water at night as with only one he is thirsty in the morning.

In addition to the daily routine for the stable-kept pony I find there are many jobs that need doing, which because they are not a daily occurrence tend to pile up or be forgotten. The way I cope with this problem is to list the tasks which need to be done and allocate them to different days. Below I have copied out the weekly timetable which I try to maintain.

**Monday:**
Skibbereen's rest day.
Lead out to graze.
Do any trimming necessary, i.e., pulling mane, tail, trimming heels etc.

**Tuesday:**
Remove cobwebs and dust from stables and tack room.

**Wednesday:**
Clean headcollar, lungeing cavesson and any other tack that is not in constant use.

**Thursday:**
Clean stirrups, bits etc. with metal polish.

**Friday:**
Wash grooming kit, tail bandages, numnahs.

# Rainy Day Bargain

**by Anne English**

**Illustrated by Heidi Best**

"Watch it when you turn off at Fennbrack corner. From there on the road to Ballcerra is hilly and very narrow," Dad shouted warningly at Mother through the half-open driving window of the van.

He had to shout to make his voice carry above the blustery keen March wind that had been blowing since early morning.

Rivulets of rain ran down from his sou'wester to mingle with those which glimmered on his oil-skin coat and cascaded from his tough Wellington boots. Mother nodded to him as my sister Polly and I waved goodbye through the steamed-up back window. The van slithered away out of the farmyard of "Tansycroft", our home. How desolate it looked, with puddles of water and mud everywhere and not an animal in sight!

But nothing could take away from the excitement we felt about going to a horse sale at Ballcerra, which this time might be the answer to our search for a Welsh pony of our own. Not even the fact that we'd already made three fruitless trips since Christmas could damp our enthusiasm. Nor were we dismayed by Mother's rueful reminder that £45 was an optimistically small sum to pay for a Welsh pony

—but it was quite definitely all we could afford.

Polly and I—she's 12 and I'm 14—just couldn't believe our parents meant it when they told us they were selling our house in Mountham and moving to a farm at the back of beyond in North Wales.

Oh, we'd known for ages that they'd had a sort of dream about wanting to get away from the smoke and grime of the city life and find a small-holding where they could keep cows, sheep, a pony or two, cultivate the land and rusticate in some old-world spot.

But we'd refused to take them seriously, even when Dad gave up his job as a teacher at Mountham Secondary Modern and enrolled at Writtle Agricultural College in Chelmsford—it's a training centre for would-be farmers—where he eventually got a diploma.

We lived in a nice comfortable flat above the flower shop which Mother owned and ran. She really had got green fingers and was marvellous at arranging flowers.

Not stiff, artificial phoney-looking arrangements, like you see at parish shows. No, hers were lovely —simple and natural to make the very best of almost every kind of flower, even daisies. Hotels were always phoning to see if she'd 'do' the flowers for weddings and other functions.

She worked awfully hard, making and selling jam, marmalade, chutney and pickles to keep things going while Dad was studying. She was forever saying how mar-vellous it would be when he qualified, and we'd be able to hunt in earnest for a place, so I suppose we shouldn't have been utterly flabbergasted when one evening she told us it was no longer just a vague idea for the never-never future, but a definite plan of action.

We loved our school, our friends, and living in a busy town like Mountham where there was tons to do on Saturdays and during the holidays.

We had smashing shops, a super indoor swimming pool, a skating rink; and we belonged to the Girl Guides, a badminton club, the local library and a children's cinema group.

"We like it here—we don't want to move to some crummy Welsh village where we don't know any-body. We're not the country type," we protested the morning the Brookfield Estate Agents sent a man to nail up a "For Sale" board on our garden fence.

"You'll love it when you settle down—and just think, you can have all the pets you've always wanted and couldn't possibly keep in a city," Mother said serenely, with a far-away look in her eyes which seemed to insulate her from properly hearing our complaints.

After that we made regular weekend dashes into Wales in our shabby Ford van, which was used for delivering flowers and plants or picking up fresh supplies for the shop.

After several unsuccessful journeys we at last found "Tansycroft".

*. . . making and selling jam, marmalade, chutney and pickles.*

It was rather a primitive-looking grey stone house flanked by a huddle of out-buildings and a granary, set in 150 acres of rough farmland.

Mother and Dad absolutely astonished us by going into raptures over it and assuring us — and each other — that it was exactly what they'd been hoping for, but hardly dared believe they'd track down.

It lay high above a valley watered by a river called the Lanna, and seven miles from Druidsdale, the nearest village.

Things moved fast after that, and while we were still grumbling and trying to get used to the forthcoming change in our lives, the shop was bought by a Mr. and Mrs. Marston, an elderly couple who wanted a joint interest for their retirement. We had to say our farewells, and one sunny June morning a huge furniture van drew up outside our gate. Four men jumped out and proceeded to pull our home to pieces and pack it into the van.

Polly and I had been given two packing cases, a week or so earlier, to stow away our special possessions. We watched miserably while these were carried out, and felt desolately that we'd never, never grow fond of alien Wales. How *could* our parents do this to us, we asked each other.

For the first couple of weeks, we stubbornly refused to take much interest in our new home. We groused about the isolation and made ourselves as awkward as possible. But during the long weeks of our summer holiday we were won over to country life. By the two beautiful collies Sally and Toss—a legacy from the Harveys who'd owned "Tansycroft" before us. By the novelty of knowing that the 20 milking cows, their 12 calves and the 120 hardy mountain sheep were *ours*.

By the quaintness of the house itself with its oak beams, inglenook fireplace, sloping ceilings and funny little hasp latches on every door.

Most of all, the freedom of being able to run wild across the fields.

Money was tight—all our available capital had been swallowed up in the new venture—and even so we'd had to get a loan from the Druidsdale Bank.

The manager took a sympathetic view of Dad's enterprise and willingly helped us out—but we knew our budget would allow no luxuries.

A milking machine was a must—and when it was installed, Polly and I never tired of watching the tangle of rubber tubing and nickel-plated nozzles being linked up to the cow's udder by Dave Griffiths, Dad's right-hand man, who was so tall and burly that Polly nicknamed him 'The Giant'.

Mother had learned to ride when she'd spent holidays at her grandmother's farm in Ireland. Just as well, because at lambing time she'd have to do a four-times-daily 100-acre patrol on horseback—most necessary on a hill farm where sheep could be buried by snow-drifts unless kept under constant vigilance.

George, a sturdy cob—another legacy from the Harveys—would be her mount. He was a nice friendly fellow, but right from the start Mother announced that her ambition was to buy a Welsh pony and try to breed from him. She infected all of us with the idea and we saved all our spare money to hoard in a box labelled PRINCE, the name he was to be called if we ever found him.

Despite the amount of work she had to do, Mother somehow made time, during the weeks before Christmas, for her favourite hobby, jewellery-making from shells, such as cornelians, amethysts and serpentines, gem stones and tiny pearls. About the last-named, she often joked, "They're my signature tune. When I'm famous, people will say: 'It's a genuine Laura Ashley—she always incorporates seed pearls in her designs'."

On the icy November evenings Polly and I helped grade the materials on the kitchen table while Mother made up necklaces, bracelets and ear-rings to sell to the arts and craft shop at Druidsdale.

They were all quickly bought by customers for Christmas presents, and the shop phoned to ask for as many more as Mother could make. Not surprising really, as they were prettier and more unusual than any we'd ever seen.

The sale at Ballcerra was taking place in a rain-sodden three-cornered meadow, bordered by dripping trees beneath which a few cars were parked. Proceedings were well underway when we arrived, as we'd been held up by the appalling weather. Some desultory bidding was in progress here and there, but attendance was poor because of the non-stop downpour.

As we munched our sandwiches, we gazed out at the gloomy scene. The heavy sky was darkening to a blackness that was full of foreboding, though it was only 4.30 p.m.

A stocky, ruddy-faced young man wearing an ankle-length mackintosh, his head covered with a wide-brimmed tweed hat, seemed exhausted as he herded together two dejected-looking creamy grey-speckled ponies.

"Obviously, the last of a number he's had for sale," said Mother,

*. . . the smaller of the two ponies . . .*

"and what a soaking he's had . . ." Suddenly she opened the door of the van. "Come on, girls—let's keep our fingers crossed—could be the rain might sway the balance in our favour." We trailed after her, sloshing through wet grass and buffeted by what was now almost a gale, until we reached the opposite hedge.

"How much are you asking for him?" enquired Mother, pointing a dripping finger at the smaller of the two ponies, to whom Polly and I had already lost our hearts.

"He's worth £60—an' more," answered their owner, bending his head and sending an avalanche of water ricocheting from his hat-brim into his eyes.

"I believe he is, but there's no use beating about the bush," replied Mother loudly in an effort to be heard above the screeching wind. "We can't afford a penny more than £45—will you take it?"

For an interminable moment the farmer's face was a study as we held our breath and—literally—prayed. Then his hand shot out to shake Mother's, then mine and finally Polly's. "Done!" he cried. "I've had my fill for one day."

We lingered only long enough to willingly pay him our precious £45 and give him our address so that he could deliver 'Prince' later in the week.

Back then to the van and to "Tansycroft". The rain was still tipping down—but it didn't bother us, for we knew it had brought us luck—forty-five-pounds worth, to be exact.

# The Young Ones

# . . . The Young Ones

62

63

Little Prince Hassan was sad. And his father, Sheik Ahmid, was also very sad. The Sheik was the boldest, fastest horseman in the whole of North Africa. One day he had been out riding his chestnut Arab stallion, Shaziman. As he cantered into the Palace yard he called over to Prince Hassan, "Come here, I think you are old enough to start riding the big horses now."

The little Prince was thrilled and rushed towards his father, but sad that he could not please him. And, of course, the Sheik was very sad because his son could not ride with him.

That summer the Sheik had to go away on business for a while and Hassan had to stay behind. One day he was out walking with his servant, Abdul, and wandered over to the market under a group of palm trees. Suddenly he heard a small voice say, "Little Prince, if you will buy me and take me home I will help you to ride again."

# The Prince And The Donkey

**by**
**Mary Holmes**

**Illustrated by Janet and Anne Grahame Johnstone**

just as he reached him he stumbled and fell right under the big horse. Poor Shaziman was startled and reared up, trampling the small boy to the ground.

The Sheik was horrified and rushed his son to the best hospital in the land. After many months little Hassan recovered, but he still had a stiff leg and whenever his father tried to coax him over to the stables he cried that he could not yet ride, and that his leg still hurt. But, really, he had been so badly frightened that he did not want to ride again. He loved his father and it made him

The Prince was startled. He looked round but saw nothing. He asked Abdul if he had heard anyone speak, but the big black man grinned and shook his head. Hassan stood still, listening, and heard the voice again: "I am over here by the second palm tree."

The Prince looked up but all he could see was a very small, very shaggy and very dirty donkey tethered to the tree. It had hairy, waving ears and a funny tail that looked like a bit of frayed old rope. But it also had inky-black mischievous eyes and long curling eyelashes. And it winked. The Prince

64

*Two white stockings, sell him to a friend;*
*Three white stockings, give him to your wife;*
*Four white stockings, ride him for your life.*

I must confess that here I can think of no explanation!

Some horses have always been highly prized because of their beautiful colour, such as the Appaloosa, whose name is derived from a breed developed by the Palouse Indians. But beware of a horse with five spots forming a circle on its hindquarters, because these markings are said to be the Devil's fingerprints!

In days gone by, funeral hearses were always pulled by teams of six or eight black horses—logical enough, since black is traditionally the colour of death and mourning. Because of this association black horses are held to be unlucky in some parts of the country, and if you meet one coming towards you it is apparently necessary to trace the sign of the cross in the air with your left forefinger in order to ward off the Evil Eye.

White or grey horses, on the other hand, are rarely regarded with such fear. Indeed, they may even be a welcome sight; the man who sees three white horses within the space of one hour is supposed to be about to come into a great fortune. An old Chinese proverb decrees that if you can think of a white horse without thinking of its tail you will soon be a very rich man. I wouldn't argue with that one!

However, if you live in Ireland white horses will not be without their sinister implications, for according to legend they are taken as mounts by the fairies for their nocturnal rides. When he came back to the ordinary world, unaged after 300 years in Tir Na Nog, Oisin had to ride everywhere on a white pony. One day he came upon two men struggling to lift a heavy sack of meal, and he dismounted to help them. The moment his foot touched the ground he became an old man.

If you stand by the side of the lake at Killarney on a windy day you will see the dancing waves crested with foam. The boatmen call these "O'Donohue's white horses"; no one is really sure just who O'Donohue was, but his spirit is supposed to glide over the waters of Killarney Lake every May-day on his favourite white horse, to the sound of unearthly music.

Horses are part of Ireland's mystery, folklore and literature. In Synge's *Riders to the Sea*, the young, strong Michael sets off to meet the Connemara boat riding on a red mare. This horse is symbolic of pulsing life and vitality, and an eerie note is struck later on when Maurya sees Michael's ghost riding on a grey pony.

Everyone has his own particular fancies and dislikes when it comes to a horse's colour; but with this, as with everything else, one man's meat is another man's poison. "Love is blind"—and so is a proud owner!

# Junior
# Jumping

1

2

1. **Vicky Gascoine and Telstar XXI competing at Hickstead. 2. Harvey Smith's son Robert riding Shropshire Lad at the Greater London Horse Show. 3. Frederick Parker with Nut Cracker. 4. Lynn Chapman with Pierrot. 5. Kelly Brown and Topcroft Tribune on their way to winning the South of England Junior Championship, 1973, at the Greater London Horse Show.**

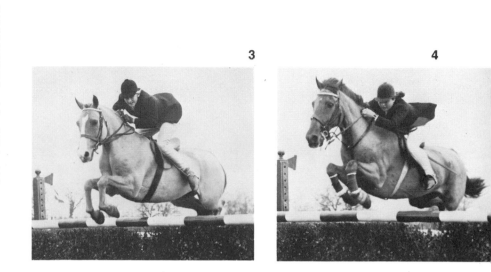

3

4

*Photos 2 and 5 by David A. Guiver*

5

83

# Bound To Fail

**by Josephine**

**Pullein-Thompson**

**Illustrated by
Christine Bousfield**

"What are the most important things to remember about feeding?" asked Jenny as they left the Ridgeway and turned down Blackley road. Pippa's mind went blank.

"Hurry up," said Jenny.

"Grass in the summer, hay in the winter and oats if they're lazy," suggested Pippa.

Jenny sighed. "You're supposed to say things like: 'always water before feeding', 'feed little and often', 'allow an hour to digest before fast work'. Now, what is the best straw for bedding?"

Pippa's mind went blank again. "I thought there was just straw, otherwise you use peat or sawdust."

"Wheat straw," Jenny told her. "You really *must* read the book, Pippa, or you'll fail *again*."

"Well, it's only silly old 'C' test," giggled Pippa. "Who cares?" But secretly she did care, very much. All her friends had passed, most of them first time, and she had failed—twice. Then she stopped dead and said, "Oh help! I've left the book at the stables. Well, that settles it; I'm bound to fail."

"I'll go back with you," Jenny offered.

"Oh we can't, not all that way," groaned Pippa. She looked at her watch. "Besides, there's no time. I promised to be home by seven."

Jenny became cold and hostile. "I'm off then," she said and turned into Chadwick Road.

I can't help it if I'm bad at things, thought Pippa, it's no use her being grumpy. Peter and Penny are clever, I've always been the stupid one of the family. No one at home minds. But it was going to be rather grim, left in the ride with the people who hadn't passed 'C' while all her friends moved up.

All through supper she was haunted by the thought of growing older and older and still being in yellow ride; and afterwards she told her mother that she simply had to go back to the stables to fetch her book.

The spring evening was warm. The gardens were dazzling with flowers and blossom and the air was scented, but Pippa was asking herself questions and barely no-ticed. It wasn't until she had left the Ridgeway and taken the drive to the stables that she realised the smell had changed and become an autumn one; fallen leaves and bonfires, she thought.

All the horses were looking out. They whinnied urgently when they saw her. That's strange, she thought; surely they've been fed? She looked over Prince's door. His haynet hung reassuringly full. There was no one about, although the three instructors lived at the stables. Christopher had a loft-like room above the office, while Maureen and Jane shared a cara-van.

Pippa went into the tack room and found her book. When she came out the bonfire smell seemed stronger and she could see smoke billowing above the lower yard where the little ponies were still stabled, waiting for the grass to grow before they were put out for the summer.

She wandered down to investi-gate, muttering the *points of the*

*horse* aloud until an extraordinary roaring noise filled her with sudden fear. She ran past the ponies' stable to the forage shed and there she saw that the great pile of hay and straw was alight and ferocious flames had just burst through and found the dry timber roof. As she watched, they roared up, growing and spreading with terrifying speed.

Dial 999, she thought, there's a telephone in the office. But as she looked from the red and roaring flames and the belching smoke to the pony stable, she knew that there wasn't time. It would only be a matter of minutes before the stable was ablaze too, and with the seven helpless ponies inside.

They stood in stalls. She ran to the far end of the long, narrow building, for it was nearest to the fire. Grey Sixpence was frightened; he whinnied nervously. Quickly she pulled the end of his rope. The

release knot undid smoothly; she dropped the wooden block on the floor, dragged the rope through the ring and hurried him out. Where could she tie him? Sparks and smoke seemed everywhere. She looked back at the stable and realised that there wasn't a second to lose, the hungry flames were already licking and darting across the small gap between the two buildings. She swung open the gate into the jumping paddock and left Sixpence to look after himself.

Patrick, a slim little bay, was trembling and the stable was hot and full of smoke. Pippa decided that she must take two. Tansy, the tiny skewbald, was already tugging at her rope and she trotted down the passageway ahead of Patrick the moment she was loosed. From the paddock Sixpence neighed anxiously. Now it was stout, square Blackberry's turn. She trod on Pippa's foot in her anxiety to get out, but there was not time to feel pain for the crackling and roaring of the flames was growing terrifyingly loud and near.

Supposing the roof falls? Pippa thought, and forced herself to say calming words in an unconcerned voice, for Minty was panicking, rearing and plunging in her stall.

"Whoa, it's all right. We'll have you out in a second," she soothed as she made grabs at the rope. The moment she was free the pony swung round, almost crushing her rescuer against the side of the stall, and fled. The stable was dark with smoke now and the heat was intense. Racked with coughing, almost blinded as smoke-induced tears poured down her face, Pippa told herself that there were only two left. Only Pepper and Carlo, she cried aloud, as she fought with her desire to run. Why didn't someone come? Instructors, grown-ups? Pepper was easy; he stood calmly and she had him out in a matter of moments, but Carlo's knot had jammed; it refused to release. She pulled with all her strength, but it wouldn't give. She tried frantically to loosen the knot, but her fingers couldn't move it. Outside there was an appalling crash followed by a fresh and more violent roaring. An orange glare dazzled her stinging eyes. The fire was almost upon them. Carlo gave a terrified whinny. Pippa fumbled blindly for his headcollar and unbuckled it. She took him by the mane and tried to lead him out. He stood stockstill, afraid to move. "You must come, quickly!" Pippa screamed at him. The heat was growing unbearable; she would be burned to death, she thought. She must leave him. Petrified with fear, the pony stood rock-like and immovable. Pippa struggled with her own terror. She snatched off her belt and slipped it round his neck. "Come on, good boy. A few steps and you'll be out in the paddock with your friends," she persuaded in a coaxing voice. Then, mercifully, one of the other ponies called to him and he found the courage to follow Pippa out.

She bundled him into the paddock and slammed the gate. Then she ran, mopping at her streaming eyes, to the office. The door wouldn't open and she struggled with it for several moments before she realised that it was locked. She was crying now with real tears; she had to get help before the fire spread. Then, suddenly, a car raced into the yard and Christopher, Maureen and Jane jumped out.

"I couldn't telephone," cried Pippa desperately, "the office is locked."

"We've sent for the fire brigade," shouted Christopher. "We saw from the hill." They ran towards the fire. Maureen was crying, "The little ponies! Oh, the poor little ponies."

"It's all right, I got them out," Pippa shouted. "They're in the jumping paddock." From the Ridgeway came the sound of sirens. She felt very tired. She remembered that she had come in for her book, and then realised that it no longer existed; she'd put it down as she untied the first pony. Well, I'm certain to fail now, she thought, as the first fire engine swept into the yard; it didn't seem very important.

She watched as the hoses were run out and torrents of water began to sluice down on the burning ruins of the lower yard.

The instructors came back. "Pippa, how did you do it?" asked Christopher. "How did you get them all out on your own?"

"You're all black and your hair's singed. It must have been terrifying," said Jane. Maureen gave her a hug and said, "Oh, I've had such a fright."

Pippa began to explain about the test and coming back for her book. "And now it's ashes," she finished, "but if someone could lend me a copy. . .?" And a sudden surge of self-confidence told her that if all her friends could pass 'C' test then so could she and, quite possibly, she'd do it tomorrow.

## Crossword Solution

### Across
1. Thoroughbred. 5. Iliad. 8. Lasso. 10. Sway. 11. Under. 13. Trace. 14. Rasp. 15. Pared. 17. Reins. 18. Liberty Horse.

### Down
1. Tail Guards. 2. Oats. 3. Gallop. 4. Red. 6. Austria. 7. Clydesdale. 9. Steeple. 12. Haynet. 16. Rear. 17. Rub.

## Pony Puzzle Answers

Dartmoor, Hackney, Shetland, Pinto, Connemara, Shire, Percheron, Lipizzaner, Morgan, Clydesdale, New Forest, Exmoor, Arab.

## Jumbled Words

1. lampas; 2. equine influenza; 3. tetanus; 4. strangles; 5. laminitis; 6. navicular; 7. fistulous withers; 8. thrush; 9. ringworm; 10. thoroughpin.

...Winter

89

**Taking a Tumble** Miss P. M. Maher and Clonrochem, from Co. Wexford, Ireland, taking a tumble during the Midland Bank Open Horse Trials at Wylye in 1973, photographed in sequence by Clive Hiles.

# 1975 Drawing Competition

The subject we have chosen for this year's competition is "At The Horse Show". This can be any type of show, from the local gymkhana to the Horse of the Year Show, and with the many aspects of show life, such as the horse-box lines, the collecting ring, the practice jump etc., you have a wide variety of scenes to choose from. Drawings, which must not be copied or traced, can be in colour or black and white, and in any medium you prefer. Before sending off your entry please read and comply with the following rules or you could be disqualified.

1. The prizes will be £3, £2 and £1 plus a number of consolation prizes according to the size and standard of entry.
2. The closing date of the competition is Friday, 17th January, 1975.
3. Competitors must not have reached their 17th birthday on that date. Age will be taken into consideration when judging this competition.
4. Write your name, age and address in BLOCK letters on the back of your entry.
5. The coupon (at the foot of this page) must be securely fixed to the entry and only one entry per coupon is allowed.
6. The Editor's decision is final and no correspondence can be entered into with regard to this competition.
7. We regret that no entries can be returned.
8. The results will be announced in the April, 1975, issue of PONY, and republished in the PONY Magazine Annual, 1976.
9. We reserve the right to publish the winning or other entries in the Annual or in PONY.
10. Address your entries to: Drawing Competition, PONY Magazine Annual 1975, Purnell Books, Berkshire House, Queen Street, Maidenhead, Berks, SL6 1NF.

*Drawing Competition*

**Pony Magazine Annual** | **1975**

**1**

**4**

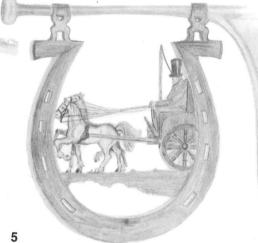

**5**

**2**

**3**

1. **JAYNE WILSON (13),**
Manor Farm, Sutton,
Nr. Peterborough,
Northants.

2. **HEIDI WEST (7), 31 Elmley**
Way, Margate, Kent.

3. **JANICE ELIZABETH**
THOMPSON (9),
Leverington Hall, Levering-
ton, Wisbech, Cambs.

4. **ALLISON ELIZABETH**
SMITH (12), 7 Waveney
Close, Hunstanton,
Norfolk.

The theme of the 1974 competition was "Horses on the Inn Sign", and it produced some highly imaginative entries — especially in the choice of name for the inn. In fact, the standard was so good that we have decided to award three extra prizes. All the winning entries, which are reproduced here (though not necessarily in order of merit), will now have received their £1 prizes.

# Competition Results

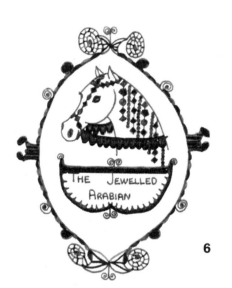

6

7

8

5. **CATRIONA REID (14),**
   6a Glasgow Road, Victoria
   Place, Milngavie, Glasgow.

6. **CAROLINE FLYNN (11),**
   Wol M.G. Flynn, 2 Div.
   Regt. RCT WKSPS (Reme),
   B.F.P.O. 46.

7. **GILLIAN TOWNLEY (15),**
   52 Church Street,
   Thurmaston, Leicester.

8. **JUNE WARDLAW (16),**
   48 Hillcrest Drive,
   Stevenston, Ayrshire,
   Scotland.